Year 4

Photocopiable
Punctuation
and Grammar

CW00460357

TOPICAL RESOURCES

Introduction

Photocopiable Punctuation and Grammar provides a variety of different activities and approaches to help Year 4 pupils understand various aspects of the English language.

It has been written with the 'Sentence Level Work' of the 'National Literacy Strategy' in mind but could be used equally as well in classes following other schemes of work.

The photocopiable pages could be used with whole classes, small groups or individual pupils at the discretion of the class teacher. They are ideal for the 'twenty minute activity time'.

Topical Resources
P.O. Box 329
Broughton
Preston
Lancashire
PR3 5LT

Topical Resources publishes a range of Educational materials for use in Primary Schools and Pre-School Nurseries and Playgroups.

For the latest catalogue:
Tel: 01772 863158
Fax: 01772 866153

E-mail sales@topical-resources.co.uk
www.topical-resources.co.uk

Copyright © 2006 Heather Bell

Illustrated by John Hutchinson

Printed in the UK for 'Topical Resources' by T. Snape & Co. Ltd., Boltons Court, Preston, Lancashire

First Published May 2006
ISBN-10 1 905509 07 3
ISBN-13 978 1 905509 07 2

Contents

Year 4
Term 1

Name: _____ Date: _____

Sentences that Make Sense

When you are writing it is important to **think out your sentence in your head first of all**. After you have written it down, read it through carefully to be sure it makes **sense** and has been **punctuated** correctly.

Task 1

Read these sentences carefully as important words are missing. Then re-write them so they make sense, using the words in the box below.

went	bought	time	swing	decided	with

1. Sam and Emma to the park. _____

2. They played on the. _____

3. Next they to buy a lolly. _____

4. They also a drink. _____

5. Later they played Joe. _____

6. At 5 o'clock it was for tea. _____

Task 2

Read each of these sentences carefully. Some of the punctuation and capital letters for proper nouns are missing. Re-write the sentences correctly.

1. "can I go to the cinema" asked tom

_____

2. we always go to mrs brown's shop to buy pies and buns

_____

3. our dogs milly and bob enjoy long walks biscuits

_____

4. did you know mr smith lives at 3 tower close

_____

5. aunt susie went shopping and bought a new dress hat coat and gloves

_____

6. "we had a lovely time" said emma

_____

Task 3

Make up **three** sentences. Write them down **without** punctuation. Ask a friend to put in the punctuation with a coloured pen or pencil.

© Topical Resources. May be photocopied for classroom use onl

Name: _____ Date: _____

Sentences that Make Sense

When you are writing, it is important **to think out your sentence in your head**. After you have written it down, read it carefully to be sure it makes **sense**, has been punctuated correctly and that **verbs and subjects agree**. For example – We **was** playing ball should read we **were** playing ball.

Task 1

Read these sentences carefully as the verbs and subjects do not agree. Re-write them correctly on the line below.

1. The twins is in bed.

_____

2. Gran and Grandad was on holiday.

_____

3. Tom were a wonderful footballer.

_____

4. Are the chocolate cake eaten?

_____

5. They was going to town on the bus.

_____

6. Anna were happy because it was her birthday.

_____

Task 2

Read this paragraph carefully putting in the correct punctuation and capital letters. There are some verbs and subjects which do not agree. Write it correctly on the lines below.

billy has four good friends sophie john beth and rajeev on saturdays they goes swimming at saltend pool afterwards they go to bennys burger bar for burger chips milkshake and an ice cream they has a great day

_____

_____

_____

_____

_____

_____

_____

Task 3

Make up three sentences of your own which need punctuation marks and capital letters. Ask a friend to correct them.

Name: _____   Date: _____

Verbs – How Much Can You Remember?

All sentences contain a verb. They can often be **action words**.
For example – The dog **barked**.

Task 1   Choose **a verb** from the box to complete the sentences.

1. The rabbit _____ the leaves.

2. The geese _____ across the farmyard.

3. Sunlight _____ through the window.

4. The giant _____ loudly when he spoke.

5. The kitten _____ the milk from the saucer.

6. The tree _____ in the breeze.

7. The boy _____ his bike.

8. The plane _____ into the sky.

waddled
swayed
shouted
soared
streamed
pedalled
lapped
nibbled

Task 2   Add more to these lists of **verbs**.

Movement Verbs	Eating Verbs	Sound Verbs	Making Verbs
jump	munch	whisper	build
run	chew	shout	construct
walk	slurp	whistle	mould
_____	_____	_____	_____
_____	_____	_____	_____
_____	_____	_____	_____
_____	_____	_____	_____
_____	_____	_____	_____
_____	_____	_____	_____
_____	_____	_____	_____

Task 3   Now use your reading book to find **16 verbs**. List them here.

_____ _____ _____ _____

_____ _____ _____ _____

_____ _____ _____ _____

_____ _____ _____ _____

     © Topical Resources. May be photocopied for classroom use onl

Name: _____ Date: _____

Verbs – Present and Past Tense

The **tense** of a verb tells us **when the event or action took place**.
For example – I am cooking – **present tense**, I cooked – **past tense**,
I will cook – **future tense**.

Task 1 *Change each sentence from the present into the past tense.*

1. He plays golf in the park. _____

2. We sing in the school play. _____

3. They jump in the sea. _____

4. She makes a cream cake. _____

5. I go to bed at 8 o'clock. _____

6. I push the baby in the pram. _____

7. I wait for a bus. _____

8. He likes his present. _____

9. They watch a film. _____

10. You build a model. _____

Task 2 *Change the verbs from the past to the present.*

Past	Present	Past	Present	Past	Present	Past	Present
swam	swim	found	_____	saw	_____	was	_____
tried	_____	knew	_____	rushed	_____	came	_____
cried	_____	broke	_____	jumped	_____	went	_____

Task 3 *Now find 8 verbs in your reading book. Write them down using the headings below.*

Past	Present	Past	Present
_____	_____	_____	_____
_____	_____	_____	_____
_____	_____	_____	_____
_____	_____	_____	_____

© Topical Resources. May be photocopied for classroom use only.

Learning Objective: to understand and use the past, present and future tense of verbs.

Name: _____   Date: _____

Verbs – Present, Past and Future Tense

The tense of a verb tells us **when the event or action took place**.
For example – I am cooking – **present tense**, I cooked – **past tense**,
I will cook – **future tense**.

Task 1   *Change each sentence from the present into the future.*

1. I catch a fish. _____

2. He washes the car. _____

3. They ring the bell. _____

4. You write a letter. _____

5. She reads a story. _____

6. We collect shells. _____

7. He brushes his teeth. _____

8. She visits the old lady. _____

9. I paint a picture. _____

10. You jump over the gate. _____

Task 2   *Complete the chart, changing each verb from the past, to present, to future tense.*

Past	-	Present	-	Future	Past	-	Present	-	Future
gave	-	give	-	will give	_____	-	_____	-	will see
talked	-	_____	-	_____	_____	-	_____	-	will play
sat	-	_____	-	_____	_____	-	go	-	_____
_____	-	hold	-	_____	_____	-	write	-	_____

Task 3   *Find the past, present and future of 6 verbs not given in this chart.*

Past	Present	Future	Past	Present	Future
_____	_____	_____	_____	_____	_____
_____	_____	_____	_____	_____	_____
_____	_____	_____	_____	_____	_____

                        © Topical Resources. May be photocopied for classroom use only

Name: _____ Date: _____

Verbs – Past, Present and Future Tense

The tense of a verb tells us **when the event or action took place**.
For example - I am cooking - **present tense**, I cooked - **past tense**,
I will cook - **future tense**.

Task 1 *Read the story carefully. Tenses have been mixed up. Write it **all in the past tense**. The **verbs** have been **highlighted** for you.*

Paresh **is** a tall, dark haired boy who **enjoys** football. One day he **is playing** for the school team when a famous footballer **saw** him. He **wants** Paresh **to train** with a professional coach. Paresh's parents **say** "yes", and soon he **is** the best player in school. His teachers **want** him to be a Premier League player one day.

_____

_____

_____

_____

_____

_____

_____

_____

_____

Task 2 *Change these sentences from the **present** to the **future**.*

1. I catch a fish.

_____

2. He washes the car.

_____

3. They ring the bell.

_____

4. You write a letter.

_____

5. She reads a story.

_____

6. We collect shells.

_____

Task 3 *Write a sentence beginning with the words and phrases given below. After each one say whether the sentence is in the **past, present** or **future**.*

1. Tomorrow _____ (_____)

2. At the present time _____ (_____)

3. Last night _____ (_____)

4. Yesterday _____ (_____)

5. Next week _____ (_____)

Topical Resources. May be photocopied for classroom use only.

Name: _____   Date: _____

Narrative Text and Past Tense

Narrative or story text is often written in the **past tense**.
For example – Neesha **explored** the gloomy, damp cave.

Task 1   *Change the story text below so that it is written in the **past tense**.*

Emma goes exploring. She hopes to find her Grandma's missing treasure. She does not look where she is going and suddenly Emma falls down a deep hole. She picks herself up and peers around in the dark. Emma pulls the torch from her pocket and shines it around. Soon she sees she is in a dark, damp cave. Behind a huge stone, she notices a shiny silver box. Emma opens it and inside there gleams rings, necklaces and other jewellery. Treasure! She has found treasure! She is very excited and runs home. Emma shows her mother the treasure. Her mother shouts to Emma's father. When he comes, he looks amazed! They lock the box in a safe.

_____

_____

_____

_____

_____

_____

_____

_____

_____

_____

_____

Task 2   *Choose a novel you enjoy. Find an exciting passage that is written in the past tense. Copy out **three sentences**. Underline the **verbs and write above them their tense**.*

_____

_____

_____

_____

_____

    © Topical Resources. May be photocopied for classroom use only.

Name: _____   Date: _____

Instruction Text and the Present Tense

Instruction text is often written in the **present tense**.
For example – **Place** the soil in the plant pot.

Task 1

*Read the following instructions. **Highlight the verb** in each one and then **cut out each sentence** and stick them in the correct order.*

How to Make a Cheese Sandwich

Cut the sandwich in half.

Take two slices of bread.

Arrange the cheese on a slice of buttered bread.

Eat and enjoy your cheese sandwich.

Place the other slice of bread on top.

Slice the cheese carefully.

Spread butter on the bread.

Task 2

*Write instructions for **one** of these in your book.*
*(**Remember to write verbs in the present tense.**)*

a. How to make a cup of coffee.
b. How to make your bed.
c. How to plant some seeds.

© Topical Resources. May be photocopied for classroom use only.

Name: _____   Date: _____

Information Text and the Present Tense

Information text has verbs which are often written in the **present tense**.

For example – Acorns **grow** on oak trees.

Task 1   *Read the following information text. The verbs are missing. Fill the gaps with a **suitable verb** that makes sense from the box below.*

lives	eat	defends	measure
built	come	search	produce

Badgers

The badger _____ in a large burrow called a sett. These creatures

_____ ninety centimetres in length. They _____ out of their sett

at dusk and _____ for food. They _____ acorns, bluebells,

blackberries and worms. The setts are tunnels _____ underground. Each

badger family _____ their territory against other badgers. They

_____ young called cubs.

*Now write a **short paragraph** in the **present tense** about another creature.*

_____

_____

_____

_____

_____

_____

_____

_____

_____

_____

    © Topical Resources. May be photocopied for classroom use only

Learning Objective: to identify and use powerful verbs.

Name: _____   Date: _____

Powerful Verbs

Writing can be made **more** exciting by choosing more **interesting verbs**.
For example: The old man **walked** into the room. This could be improved by
changing the verb to a more interesting one. The old man **shuffled** into the
room.

Task 1   *Highlight the verb in each of these sentences and then replace it with a more exciting one from the box below.*

slithered	limped	leaped	screeched	escaped	ordered

1. The monkey jumped out of the tree.

_____

2. The snake crawled over the stone.

_____

3. The injured dog walked to the top of the hill.

_____

4. The frightened boy shouted for help at the top of his voice.

_____

5. The thief got away.

_____

6. The teacher told the boy to sit down.

_____

Task 2   *Sort out these **muddled words** to make a **powerful verb which means the same as the one in brackets**. The first one is done for you.*

tpeal **leapt** (jumped)   thae _____ (dislike)

pecsade _____ (got out)   bobsde _____ (cried)

dehwspire _____ (spoke quietly)   retnede _____ (went in)

bltrmee _____ (shake)   reasch _____ (to look for)

Task 3   *Now find some powerful verbs in your reading book.*

Topical Resources. May be photocopied for classroom use only.

Name: _____   Date: _____

Powerful Verbs

Writing can be made more exciting by choosing more interesting verbs.
For example: The old man **walked** into the room. This could be improved
by changing the verb to a more interesting one. The old man **shuffled**
into the room.

Task 1   *Re-write this short story on the lines below **changing the verbs highlighted** for **more interesting ones**.*

One sunny afternoon, Sam and Beth **were walking** in the park. They saw a squirrel
and **running** after it was a large black cat. The squirrel **looked** quite **frightened**.
The cat tried to **jump** on it. Luckily the squirrel **got away** by **going up** a nearby
tree. The cat **sat** and **looked up** at the squirrel in anger. The squirrel **had been
able** to get away.

_____

_____

_____

_____

_____

_____

_____

_____

Task 2   *Highlight the verb in each of these sentences and then **replace it with a more exciting one**. Write it on the short line following the sentence.*

1. The angry bull ran around the field. _____

2. We found the treasure. _____

3. The boy drank his juice. _____

4. The mouse bit at the cheese. _____

5. The elephant walked on the leaves. _____

6. The girl cried when she fell over. _____

7. The dog jumped into the air. _____

8. Sally talked to her friend. _____

    © Topical Resources. May be photocopied for classroom use only

Learning Objective: to understand adverbs and their use in sentences.

Name: _____   Date: _____

Adverbs

Adverbs tell us more about the verb in a sentence. They explain **how** something happened. They often end in **'ly'**.
For example – The man sang **loudly**.

Task 1   *Look at what is happening in each picture, then write a sentence with an adverb ending in 'ly'. In the last two boxes **draw a picture** to explain the sentences.*

The cat pounced quickly.

_____
_____

_____
_____

_____
_____

_____

The boy danced gracefully.

_____

The girl ate greedily.

Task 2   *Put **a ring around an adverb** to complete each sentence so that it makes sense.*

1. The bull charged (angrily/silently) across the field.

2. The mouse crept (strongly/quietly) into the room.

3. The tortoise walked (slowly/quickly) up the garden path.

4. The bird sang (stupidly/sweetly).

5. Tom did his sums (correctly/heavily).

6. Mum iced the cake (gently/carefully).

7. The lady shouted (loudly/cheerfully).

8. The dog growled (fiercely/happily).

9. The baby laughed (silently/happily).

Topical Resources. May be photocopied for classroom use only.

Name: _____ Date: _____

Collecting Adverbs

Adverbs tell us more about verbs. They explain how something happened. Adverbs often end in **'ly'**.
For example – The bird sang **sweetly**.

Task 1 *Complete the table below with **adverbs which end in 'ly'**.*

Classifying Adverbs

sounds	speeds	feelings
loudly	quickly	sadly
_____	_____	_____
_____	_____	_____
_____	_____	_____
_____	_____	_____

Task 2 *Write a paragraph about '**A Visit to the Zoo**.
Use as many of the **adverbs** in the box below as possible.*

loudly	cheekily	greedily	happily	speedily
angrily	suddenly	silently	slowly	immediately

_____

_____

_____

_____

_____

_____

_____

_____

_____

_____

_____

_____

18 © Topical Resources. May be photocopied for classroom use only

Name: _____   Date: _____

Adverbs

Adverbs tell us more about verbs. They explain how something happened.
Adverbs often end in 'ly'.
For example – The bird sang sweetly.

Task 1   *Using **an adverb that ends in 'ly' from the box**, complete these sentences.*

1. The thief climbed _____ in the open window.

2. The boy laughed _____ at the joke.

3. The teacher shouted _____ at the naughty boy.

4. The lady whispered _____ to her friend.

5. The baby slept _____ in the pram.

6. The elephant stamped _____ in the mud.

soundly
angrily
heavily
quietly
loudly
quickly

Task 2   *Highlight the adverbs in this paragraph. Then choosing **four** of them, write a **sentence** using each on the lines below.*

The Prince boldly knocked at the castle door.

"Is no one in?" he shouted grumpily.

Slowly the door opened and an old lady asked anxiously, "What do you want?"

"I'd like to speak to the King," the young man said firmly.

The old lady answered sadly that the King no longer lived there.

"Run away quickly," she said, "or the giant who lives here will happily eat you for his tea."

1. _____

_____

2. _____

_____

3. _____

_____

4. _____

_____

© Topical Resources. May be photocopied for classroom use only.

Name: _____ Date: _____

Adverbs

Adverbs tell us more about verbs. They explain how something has happened. Adverbs often end in **'ly'**.
For example – The birds sang sweetly.

Task 1 *Read the passage carefully. **Change the adverbs for different ones**, so the story still makes sense.*

Tom marched [_____] up the lane. In the trees the birds sang
quickly

[_____] and the sheep munched [_____] at the long grass.
merrily   happily

[_____] Tom heard someone screaming [_____]!
Suddenly   madly

[_____] he saw a bull chasing [_____] after a man who
Immediately   fiercely

was running [_____] across the field. [_____] Tom opened
quickly   Quickly

the gate [_____] so the man could run [_____] out of the
carefully   hastily

bull's way. The man shouted [_____], "You saved my life!"
gratefully

Task 2 *Use each of these **adverbs** in a short sentence to show their meaning.*

| quickly | clearly | carefully | gladly | possibly | proudly |

_____

_____

_____

_____

_____

_____

Task 3 *Now find **six adverbs** in your reading book.*

  © Topical Resources. May be photocopied for classroom use only

Learning Objective: to understand the purpose of adverbs and that alternatives can be used.

Name: _____   Date: _____

Adverbs

Adverbs tell us something more about verbs. They explain how something happened. Adverbs often end in **'ly'**.

For example – The bird sang **sweetly**.

Task 1   *Complete these sentences in **three different ways**, so that the sentence makes sense.*

The boy spoke _____   The man chatted _____
                _____   _____
                _____   _____

Priya replied _____   The boy ate _____
                _____   _____
                _____   _____

The old lady smiled _____   The Princess danced _____
                      _____   _____
                      _____   _____

Task 2   *Look at the picture. Write **six sentences** about it on the lines below. Each sentence should contain **at least one adverb**.*

_____

_____

_____

_____

_____

_____

© Topical Resources. May be photocopied for classroom use only.

Name: _____ Date: _____

Adverbs with Similar Meanings

Adverbs tell us something more about verbs. They explain how something happened. Adverbs often end in **'ly'**.
For example – The bird sang **sweetly**.

Task 1   *Find the **pairs of adverbs which have similar meanings**. Write them on the line below.*

cheerfully	sadly	cleverly	noisily
neatly	silently	honestly	rudely
impolitely	truthfully	noiselessly	sorrowfully
tidily	intelligently	loudly	happily

honestly   truthfully
_____   _____

_____   _____

_____   _____

_____   _____

Task 2   *Read the paragraph below. **Underline the adverbs**, then re-write the passage using other adverbs of similar meaning.*

Gopal and Sammy walked swiftly down the path to school. They opened the door quietly. It was strangely quiet, "Where is everyone?" Gopal shouted loudly.
"Can I help you?" a voice asked sweetly. Seeing it was the Headteacher, Sammy asked shyly where the other children had gone.
"Haven't you guessed?" she said kindly.
"Oh no," said Gopal tiredly, "it's the special holiday!"

_____

_____

_____

_____

_____

_____

_____

_____

_____

_____

 © Topical Resources. May be photocopied for classroom use only.

Name: _____   Date: _____

Commas

A comma often separates different parts of a sentence.
It shows us when to pause when we are reading.
For example – As it was raining, we stayed in at playtime.

Task 1   *Decide where the comma needs to go in these sentences and write them on the line below.*

1. During the winter we stay in after tea.

   _____

2. After dinner I must do my homework.

   _____

3. From out of the egg a small chick hatched.

   _____

4. Looking very lovely the bride waved to the crowd.

   _____

5. After waiting for an hour finally the bus came.

   _____

6. Even though Tom is only six he plays wonderful cricket.

   _____

Task 2   Complete these sentences.

1. During the night, _____

2. After his breakfast, _____

3. Speeding down the road, _____

4. Hoping to win a prize, _____

5. After walking to his Gran's house, _____

6. Breathing fire, _____

Task 3   *Find an example of this use of the comma in your reading book. Write it here.*

_____

© Topical Resources. May be photocopied for classroom use only.   23

Learning Objective: to practise using commas to mark grammatical boundaries in sentences.

Name: _____ Date: _____

Commas to Mark Clauses

A comma often separates different parts of a sentence. It shows us when to pause when we are reading. They sometimes mark out **relative clauses** that slot into a sentence to give us **extra information**. For example – Laura, who is my cousin, came to tea.

Task 1   *Add extra information into these sentences **using commas to separate the clause.** The first one has been done for you.*

1. The swimming teacher is my neighbour. (who is called Mr Brown)

   The swimming teacher, who is called Mr Brown, is my neighbour.
   _____

2. I could win first prize at the talent show. (if I try hard)
   _____

3. At the zoo the parrot escaped. (a beautiful bird)
   _____

4. The oak tree was blown down. (the tallest tree in the wood)
   _____

5. Glasgow is in Scotland. (a large city)
   _____

6. The lovely jug is very valuable. (an antique)
   _____

Task 2   *Complete these sentences by **adding a relative clause**.*

1. The old lady, _____ , is ninety today.

2. At the football match, _____ , I saw my Uncle John.

3. The shop, _____ , was closed.

4. My friend, _____ ,is a wonderful singer.

5. Our school, _____ , has two hundred pupils.

6. My favourite book, _____ , was on the shelf.

7. The teacher, _____ , is a swimming champion.

8. My Aunt Joan, _____ , has three dogs.

 © Topical Resources. May be photocopied for classroom use only.

Year 4
Term 2

Learning Objective: to revise the function of adjectives in sentences.

Name: _____   Date: _____

Adjectives

Adjectives tell us more about nouns. They are **describing words**.
For example – a **beautiful** princess.

Task 1   *Choose a **suitable adjective** from the box below to complete these phrases.*

| old | exciting | sparkling | snappy | delicious | fierce |
| empty | handsome | loud | dark | tuneful | juicy |

a [   ] pear   an [   ] lady   a [   ] dog

a [   ] lion   an [   ] adventure   an [   ] cup

a [   ] diamond   a [   ] prince   a [   ] meal

a [   ] noise   a [   ] night   a [   ] song

Task 2   *Ring the **adjectives** in this paragraph.*

The tall, handsome prince rode on his beautiful, black horse into the dark, deep

wood. All around he heard the strange sounds. The shrill hoot of the owl, the

rustling noise of tall trees swaying in the wind. Then suddenly he saw it! A golden

castle with a huge wooden door appeared before him. This was where the beautiful

princess lived with her wise father.

Task 3   *Now choose **five** of the adjectives and use them in sentences of your own.*

(1) _____

(2) _____

(3) _____

(4) _____

(5) _____

    © Topical Resources. May be photocopied for classroom use only.

Learning Objective: to revise the function of adjectives in sentences.

Name: _____   Date: _____

Adjectives

Adjectives tell us more about nouns. They are describing words.
For example – a **beautiful** princess

Task 1

The adjective 'nice' has been used in these phrases. It tells us very little about the noun. Change it for a more suitable and interesting adjective.

a nice apple
_____

a nice chair
_____

a nice garden
_____

a nice smell
_____

a nice present
_____

a nice tune
_____

a nice sunset
_____

a nice neighbour
_____

nice handwriting
_____

a nice puppy
_____

Task 2

*Pick out the **adjective** in these phrases and replace it with one which means the **opposite**.*

a beautiful house
_____

a modern painting
_____

a glossy magazine
_____

a filthy cup
_____

a rough piece of wood
_____

a wealthy man
_____

an ugly witch
_____

a stupid answer
_____

a strong lady
_____

a priceless vase
_____

Task 3   *Find 8 adjectives in your reading book.*

_____ _____ _____ _____

_____ _____ _____ _____

© Topical Resources. May be photocopied for classroom use only.

Learning Objective: to understand and use adjectives in similes.

Name: _____ Date: _____

Similes

Similes compare a subject to something else. They help to describe a subject more clearly and often contain an adjective.

For example – as quiet as a mouse

Task 1 *Match the **correct beginnings and endings** to each of these similes. Write them on the lines below.*

Beginnings	Endings
as fierce	as a snail
as busy	as a gorilla
as fast	as a lion
as gentle	as an owl
as hairy	as a bee
as proud	as a hare
as slow	as a lamb
as wise	as a peacock

as fierce as a lion _____ _____

_____ _____

_____ _____

_____ _____

Task 2 *Complete these similes.*

as flat as _____ as clean as _____

as bitter as _____ as cool as _____

as poor as _____ as angry as _____

as slippery as _____ as white as _____

as graceful as _____ as clear as _____

Task 3 *Now look through a story book and see if you can find any similes. If you cannot find any, then make some up of your own. Write them on the lines below.*

_____ _____

_____ _____

_____ _____

_____ _____

    © Topical Resources. May be photocopied for classroom use only.

Learning Objective: to understand and use adjectives in similes.

Name: _____ Date: _____

Similes

Similes compare a subject to something else. They help to describe a subject more clearly and often contain an adjective.
For example – as quiet as a mouse

Task 1   *Circle the similes in this paragraph.*

Sam was as happy as a king. He had just been on holiday and was as brown as a berry. He and his dad had flown on a plane and quick as lightening they arrived in Spain. Sam swam in the pool every day and felt as fit as a fiddle. He bought presents for his friends and his case was as heavy as an elephant when he returned home. Sam must have been as strong as an ox to carry it. They both said the holiday was fun and they felt as fresh as a daisy on their return.

Task 2   *Sometimes similes become dull because they are used too often. Make up some new, exciting ones of your own. The first one is done for you.*

as dark as a velvety night sky.

as quiet as _____

as happy as _____

as tall as _____

as fierce as _____

as old as _____

as white as _____

as ugly as _____

as hot as _____

as frightened as _____

as fresh as _____

as hairy as _____

as strong as _____

Task 3   *Make a collection of similes from books, poems and from people you know.*

_____

_____

_____

_____

_____

Learning Objective: to understand adjectival phrases and be able to use them.

Name: _____   Date: _____

Adjectival Phrases

An **adjectival phrase** contains several words which **tell us more about a noun**. Adjectival phrases contain **more than just a single adjective**.
For example – The singer was **absolutely amazing**!

Task 1

Read each of these sentences carefully.
Circle the adjectival phrases.

1. The witch's nails were sharp black claws.
2. The bird flew into the cloudless blue sky.
3. It was a fantastically exciting film.
4. Tara walked into the frighteningly dark room.
5. The baby was as good as gold.
6. He is an extremely clever boy.
7. The tramp had dirty smelly clothes.
8. The truly graceful princess waved at the crowd.
9. It was an amazing gripping story.

Task 2

*Complete these **adjectival phrases**.*

1. The _____ _____ prince broke down the door.
2. The book is _____ _____ and _____.
3. It was a _____ _____ day.
4. The _____ and _____ path leads to the woods.
5. The old lady gave me a _____ _____ smile.
6. The nurse was a kind _____ person.
7. The play was _____ _____ and long.
8. The snake moved _____ along the path.

Task 3

*Look in your reading book and try to find **3 adjectival phrases**.*
Alternatively, make up 3 of your own.

_____

_____

_____

                                    © Topical Resources. May be photocopied for classroom use only.

Name: _____ Date: _____

Comparative and Superlative Adjectives

When we compare nouns we use **comparative adjectives**. These can often **end in 'er'**.
For example – Sam is **taller** than Rajeev.
When we compare **more than two nouns we use superlative adjectives**. These often **end in 'est'**.
For example – Emma is the **tallest** in the whole class.

Task 1 Complete the **comparative and superlative adjectives below**.

Positive	Comparative	Superlative
tall	taller	tallest
fast	_____	_____
late	_____	_____
small	_____	_____
weak	_____	_____
brave	_____	_____
strong	_____	_____
young	_____	_____
old	_____	_____

Task 2 Complete these sentences using **either** a comparative **or** superlative adjective.

1. Sara is the _____ of the two girls. (tall)

2. The greyhound is the _____ of all the dogs. (fast)

3. Priya is the _____ girl in the school (clever)

4. Hamid is the _____ boy in Cubs. (strong)

5. John was the _____ of the two soldiers. (brave)

6. Jane is _____ than her friend Anna. (polite)

7. The _____ to arrive in our class is William. (late)

8. James climbed _____ than John. (high)

© Topical Resources. May be photocopied for classroom use only.

Name: _____ Date: _____

Comparative and Superlative Adjectives

Adjectives ending in 'e' - in the comparative form **add 'er'** and in the **superlative form add 'est'**.
For example – late, lat**er**, lat**est**.
Two syllable adjectives ending in 'y', change the 'y' to 'i' when adding er and est.
For example – sunny, sunn**ier**, sunn**iest**.

Task 1   *Complete the table below.*

Positive	Comparative	Superlative
white		
	funnier	
		happiest
	safer	
brave		
		hungriest
	stormier	
		latest
lucky		

Task 2   *Complete these sentences using these **irregular adjectives**.*

Here are some common adjectives which have **irregular comparatives and superlatives**.

Positive	Comparative	Superlative
good	better	the best
bad	worse	the worst
much/many	more	the most
little	less	the least

1. Amber's work was good but Amy's was _____.

2. Laura's work was _____ _____ in the class.

3. Billy ate _____ than Tom, but Adam ate the most.

4. Gopal did very little work. His friend James did less but Finlay did

_____ _____.

5. Sally's painting was _____ but Jim's was better.

© Topical Resources. May be photocopied for classroom use only.

Learning Objective: to understand the use of adverbs used with adjectives to show degree of intensity.

Name: _____ Date: _____

Comparative and Superlative Adjectives

When an **adjective is a long one**, it can often sound odd to add 'er' or 'est'. **It sounds right when we use the adverbs more or most instead of these endings**. For example – Beth looks worried but Jack looks **more** worried. Hayley looks the **most** worried of all.

Task 1

Complete the table of adjectives below.
*Sometimes we use **more** or most rather than adding **er** or **est** to the adjective. Think carefully which sounds correct.*

Positive	Comparative	Superlative
short		
	more important	
		most beautiful
	more handsome	
far		
	greater	
		most comfortable
	more generous	

Task 2

*More refers to **two things** and **most** refers to **more than two**. Complete these sentences by choosing **either more or most**.*

1. Who ate _____ dinner; Susie, Emma or Rachel?

2. Which do you enjoy _____ ; History or Geography?

3. Jake works harder than David, but David has _____ ability.

4. Read all the pages in the catalogue and choose the toy you like _____.

5. Who has _____ homework; Anna or Peter?

6. In the spelling test, Sara gained the _____ marks in the class.

7. Out of all of your presents, which do you like _____ ?

8. In netball, our team gained _____ goals than the other team.

© Topical Resources. May be photocopied for classroom use only.

Name: _____   Date: _____

Using Apostrophes to Show Possession

Apostrophes can be used to show possession (that something belongs to someone).
The rule for adding apostrophes depends on the noun or person to which it is being added. If **the noun is singular and does not end in 's' then add an apostrophe and an 's'**. For example – the girl's cat
If the noun is singular and ends in an 's' you add an apostrophe and an 's'. For example – the boss's car.

Task 1   *Match each sentence with its meaning. The first one has been done for you.*

the lady's hat	the wing belonging to the bird
the mouse's tail	**the hat belonging to the lady**
the bird's wing	the tail belonging to the mouse
the baby's pram	the brush belonging to the artist
the artist's brush	the pram belonging to the baby
the cook's hat	the hat belonging to the cook

Task 2   *Write a shorter form of these using an apostrophe.*

1. The tail belonging to the dog.   _____

2. The pencil belonging to the child.   _____

3. The mane belonging to the horse.   _____

4. The cover belonging to the book.   _____

5. The boots belonging to the lady.   _____

6. The egg belonging to the duck.   _____

7. The watch belonging to Tom.   _____

8. The phone belonging to Emma.   _____

Task 3   *Now find **three examples** of the **use of an apostrophe to show possession** in your reading book. Write them on the lines below.*

_____   _____   _____

     © Topical Resources. May be photocopied for classroom use only.

Name: _____   Date: _____

Using Apostrophes to Show Possession

Apostrophes can be used to show possession (that something belongs to someone).
The rule for adding apostrophes depends on the noun or person to which it is being added.
If the noun is singular and does not end in 's' then add an apostrophe and an 's'.
For example – the girl's cat
If the noun is singular and ends in an 's' you add an apostrophe and an 's'.
For example – the boss's car
If the noun is plural and ends in 's' you add an apostrophe but do not add an 's'.
For example – the workers' tools
If the noun is plural and doesn't end in an 's' then you add an apostrophe and an 's'.
For example – the men's hats

Task 1   *Match each sentence with its meaning. The first one has been done for you.*

the men's coats	the nests belonging to the wasps
the boy's shoe	the parents belonging to the princess
the wasps' nests	the toys belonging to the babies
the princess's parents	the shoe belonging to the boy
the farmers' sheep	the sheep belonging to the farmers
the babies' toys	**the coats belonging to the men**

Task 2   *Re-write these sentences using **apostrophes**.*

1. The womens coats are here. _____

2. We played with Sams dog. _____

3. Over there is the Pets Corner. _____

4. The ponys tail is brown. _____

5. Here is the bosss car. _____

6. I enjoy childrens books. _____

7. The flies wings were broken. _____

Task 3   *Now find four place names which have apostrophes in them. For example – St Paul's Cathedral. Write them on the lines below.*

_____   _____   _____   _____

© Topical Resources. May be photocopied for classroom use only.   **35**

Learning Objective: to understand that apostrophes can be used to show possession.

Name: _____   Date: _____

Using Apostrophes to Show Possession

We use apostrophes to show that something belongs to someone (possession).
For example – The girl's dog (the dog belonging to the girl)
The girls' dog. (the dog belonging to more than one girl)

Task 1   *The apostrophes are missing from the sentences below. **Mark them in red in the correct place**.*

1. Marys poem was the best in her group.
2. The cats kitten was lost.
3. The babies crying filled the room.
4. The suns rays shone brightly.
5. The Princes servant came to the door.
6. The childrens swing was broken.
7. The mens hats blew away.
8. The birds egg hatched.
9. The womens meeting finished early.
10. The foxs den was hard to find.

Task 2   *Explain each of these phrases. The first two have been done for you.*

1. The tiger's stripes   The stripes belonging to the tiger
2. The teachers' classrooms   The classrooms belonging to the teachers
3. The ladies' dresses _____
4. The spider's web _____
5. The rabbits' ears _____
6. The clown's hat _____
7. Sam's house _____
8. My cousins' house _____
9. The horses' hooves _____
10. The dog's tail _____

Task 3   *Make up **three sentences** which need apostrophes. Ask a friend to put in the apostrophes.*

    © Topical Resources. May be photocopied for classroom use only.

Learning objective: to understand and use the apostrophe in contractions.

Name: _____   Date: _____

Apostrophes for Contractions

Words can be shortened by missing out letters. These are called **contractions** and the **apostrophe is used to show us where the letter is missing**.
For example – didn't – did not

Task 1 *Explain in full the meaning of each of these **contractions**.*

hasn't	has not	we've	
can't		I'm	
wouldn't		she'll	
you're		he's	
I'll		mustn't	

Task 2 *Write these words as **contractions**.*

I have		it is	
she is		they are	
could not		he will	
we have		does not	
should not		had not	

Task 3 *There are **eight contractions** in this paragraph. **Circle them** and **list them below** and **say what each stands for**. The first one has been done for you.*

Dear Emma,
I hope you've received my last letter. If you didn't then it doesn't matter too much as we're coming to visit you. We'll be staying for the week and I've asked Dad if he'll let me stay longer. Weren't we lucky our holidays were the same!
See you soon,
Sally

you've = you have	

Ⓒ Topical Resources. May be photocopied for classroom use only.

Name: _____   Date: _____

Word Order in Sentences

Word order in sentences is very important. Changing word order
can make a sentence lose its meaning.
For example – 'Neesha ate a large fish.'
This could be changed to - 'A large fish ate Neesha.'
Sometimes re-ordering the words in a sentence can change the meaning.
'Neesha saw a snake.' This could change to - 'A snake saw Neesha.'

Task 1   *Re-arrange the words in these sentences so that they make sense.*

1. had The boy dog. a

2. starts School at nine o'clock.

3. enjoy playing football. I

4. built of bricks. was The house

5. a good cook. My is Dad

6. capital The Paris. of is France

7. are There in a week. seven days

8. a pound. make One hundred pence

Task 2   *Re-arrange these sentences so that the meaning is changed.*

1. The spider caught a giant fly.

2. The plane crashed into the train.

3. The man was chased by a lion.

4. Bobby ate the large octopus.

5. Sam spoke to the Queen.

6. Ahmed sat on the horse.

7. Carly peeped at the baby.

8. The dog bit the cat

Task 3   *Make up three sentences of your own which can be re-arranged to change their meaning. Ask a friend to re-arrange them.*

_____

_____

_____

_____

    © Topical Resources. May be photocopied for classroom use only.

Learning Objective: to understand how conjunctions are used to join sentences.

Name: _____ Date: _____

Joining Sentences

A conjunction is a joining word. Two short sentences can be **joined together** to make a longer one by using a conjunction.
For example - **John threw the ball. Jo caught it.** - could become -
John threw the ball and Jo caught it.

Task 1   *Join these two short sentences together using one of the conjunctions in the box below.*

so	as	but	until	when	and

1. Sally sings loudly. Aftab sings even more loudly.
   _____

2. It rained all day. We had to play inside.
   _____

3. The boy was sick. He had eaten too much.
   _____

4. I jumped out of bed. I heard the alarm.
   _____

5. We waited at the window. Granny arrived in her car.
   _____

6. I like cod. I like haddock.
   _____

Task 2   *Put a ring around the conjunctions, then split these sentences into two short ones.*

1. I made tea while my brother did his homework.
   _____

2. The car skidded as the snow made the road slippy.
   _____

3. We played Ludo after we helped wash up.
   _____

4. The teacher was pleased because the class had won the prize.
   _____

5 I went to the shop but it had closed.
   _____

6. Sam went to the party although he did not want to.
   _____

Task 3   *Find two sentences in your reading book which could be joined into a longer one.*

   _____
   _____

© Topical Resources. May be photocopied for classroom use only.

Name: _____   Date: _____

Joining Sentences

A conjunction is a joining word. Two short sentences can be **joined together** to make a longer one by using a **conjunction.** For example - **John threw the ball. Jo caught it**. - could become **John threw the ball and Jo caught it.**

Task 1

*Make up a sensible **beginning** to these sentence endings. **Circle** the **conjunction**.*

1. _____ after we have our dinner.

2. _____ before you go to bed.

3. _____ unless Mum agrees.

4. _____ if you have time.

5. _____ because he was ill.

6. _____ while you are learning your spellings.

7. _____ although she is only six.

8. _____ but I am good at football.

Task 2

*Now make up a sensible **ending** for each of these sentences. **Circle** the **conjunction**.*

1. They worked so late that _____ .

2. Tom didn't want to go to his Aunt's because _____ .

3. Ahmed was upset until _____ .

4. The thieves put the gold bars in a van as _____ .

5. The little boy left the house after _____ .

6. Mary put on her favourite jumper and _____ .

7. The old lady screamed when _____ .

8. I washed the dishes so _____ .

Task 3

Find three long sentences which contain conjunctions in your reading book and write them below. Underline the conjunctions.

_____

_____

_____

          © Topical Resources. May be photocopied for classroom use only.

Name: _____   Date: _____

Complex Sentences – Using Conjunctions

Complex sentences can be made by **joining two simple sentences with a conjunction**. For example: I have a dog. I also have a cat. - could become - **I have a dog and I also have a cat**.

Task 1 *Read the pairs of sentences carefully. Make them into a **complex sentence** by joining them with one of the **conjunctions** below. The first one is done for you.*

while	but	and	so	as	before	after	though

1. I like football. I also like cricket.
   _____

2. Tim loves pizza. He hates chicken pie.
   _____

3. I have some cocoa. I go to bed.
   _____

4. Ahmed went to school. First he went to the dentist.
   _____

5. Jon is tall. He reached the box on the top shelf.
   _____

6. Emma ran inside. It began to rain.
   _____

7. I cannot ride a bike. I have tried hard to learn.
   _____

8. Sammy listened to the radio. He did his homework.
   _____

Task 2 *The **wrong** conjunction has been used to join these sentences. **Replace the wrong conjunction with the correct one**.*

1. Neesha fell off the swing until she was going too fast.
   _____

2. Tom was given a computer although it was his Christmas present.
   _____

3. We went to feed the stray cat because it had gone away.
   _____

4. I cannot swim because I cannot ski.
   _____

5. She went to bed although she was tired.
   _____

© Topical Resources. May be photocopied for classroom use only.

Name: _____   Date: _____

Complex Sentences – Using Adverbials

An adverbial is a group of words that are used in the same way as an adverb. We can make more interesting complex sentences by using these to give us more information. For example - Before the play, we went out for tea. Before the play, is the adverbial. It is divided off from the rest of the sentence by a comma.

Task 1   *Here are some **adverbials**. **Complete** each sentence **so it makes sense**.*

1. After the match, _____

2. During the lesson, _____

3. Before our holiday, _____

4. When the thief broke in, _____

5. As we walked home, _____

6. While Ben was out, _____

7. Before I go to bed, _____

8. During the school visit, _____

9. After my birthday, _____

10. When we went to France, _____

Task 2   *Now make up some adverbials to make each sentence make sense. Don't forget to divide it off from the rest of the sentence with a comma.*

1. _____ we went to visit my Aunt.

2. _____ I always have a shower.

3. _____ they saw a squirrel in the tree.

4. _____ one of the actors fainted.

5. _____ I put on my shorts.

6. _____ the children played in the garden.

7. _____ we went to the cinema.

8. _____ they spotted an eagle.

9. _____ we went into town.

10. _____ Susan wrote a thank you letter.

   © Topical Resources. May be photocopied for classroom use only.

Name: _____   Date: _____

Complex Sentences

Another way of joining sentences, is to move the verb to the beginning of the sentence. For example – **Mum sat by the fire. She began to read the paper**. This could be changed into one sentence. **Sitting down by the fire, Mum began to read the paper**. Notice how a comma is used to separate off the first part of the sentence.

Task 1   *Join these sentences in the same way . **Don't forget to use a comma**.*

1. We walked in the park. We met our friend Rajeev.

   Walking in _____

2. I stood by the shop. I saw the van unload the goods.

   Standing _____

3. He came home early. He found the door locked.

   _____

4. Sarah arrived at the school. She talked to her friend.

   _____

5. They walked in the fields. They saw a bull.

   _____

6. They climbed the mountain. They had a wonderful view.

   _____

7. He arrived at the finish line. Peter had won the race.

   _____

8. He listened to the radio. Dad made tea.

   _____

Task 2   *Now **complete** these sentences **so they make sense**.*

1. Opening the present, Sam _____

2. Playing football in the park, they _____

3. Arriving in Spain, we _____

4. Travelling on the bus, Halim _____

5. Walking in the woods, Mr Smith _____

6. Climbing to the top, they _____

© Topical Resources. May be photocopied for classroom use only.

Year 4

Term 3

Name: _____   Date: _____

Verb Endings or Suffixes

A group of letters such as 'ing' or 'ed' can be added to **the end of a verb**.
For example – Jim is play**ing** football or Jim play**ed** football. The **'ed' or 'ing'**
ending tells us more about **when the action took place**, in the present or
past.

Task 1   *Re-write these sentences, using the **correct verbs**, on the line below. **Underline the** **suffix** added to the verb to make it correct.*

1. Yesterday, Mr and Mrs Brown call at their son's house.
   Yesterday, Mr and Mrs Brown called at their son's house.
   _____

2. Today, the teacher is teach the class.
   _____

3. "I hope the children behave well," asked the Headteacher.
   _____

4. I am cook an omelette this afternoon.
   _____

5. Susie always want to go to the zoo.
   _____

6. "Are you come to tea?" asked Emma.
   _____

7. The dogs were chase each other in the garden.
   _____

8. Tomorrow we will be go on holiday.
   _____

Task 2   *Add **suffixes** to the highlighted verbs in the letter so that they make sense. Write them on the lines below.*

Dear Jamila,

I am **write** to ask if you are **come** to stay soon. Mum has **promise** to take us **shop**
in the city. When we have **look** around the shops and have **pick** something we want,
she will take us for lunch. I am **hope** that she might take us to a Chinese restaurant.
She said if we **want** to we could then go to the fair. Let me know if you are
definitely **come**. I have **save** all my pocket money for us to spend.
Lots of love,
Maria.

_____   _____   _____   _____   _____

_____   _____   _____   _____   _____

   © Topical Resources. May be photocopied for classroom use only.

Name: _____   Date: _____

Making Plurals – Words Ending in 'Y'

When making a word ending **in 'y' into a plural, look at the letter before the 'y'. If the letter before the 'y' is a vowel, just add 's'** – donkey > donkeys.
If it is a consonant change 'y' to 'i' and add 'es' – lady > ladies.

Task 1   *Apply this rule to the words below and write their plural.*

journey	penny	story	valley
_____	_____	_____	_____
monkey	ruby	kidney	spy
_____	_____	_____	_____
toy	enemy	fly	holiday
_____	_____	_____	_____
dictionary	body	fairy	trolley
_____	_____	_____	_____
bully	display	abbey	cherry
_____	_____	_____	_____

Task 2   *Re-write the following passage making all the nouns highlighted plural. Remember to think carefully about plurals of words ending in 'y'.*

When we were on our **holiday** there was a **cherry** tree in the garden. We had lots of **opportunity** to pick them. Sometimes a **fly** would land on them. "Don't let the **baby** have one!" Mum shouted. "Tell her a **story** about a **fairy** to keep her happy!" One day at the zoo, we took her to see a **monkey, a donkey, a pony** and **a bunny.** She liked the **puppy** best.

_____

_____

_____

_____

_____

_____

_____

Task 3   *Look through some books. Can you find some more plurals which follow these rules? Write them on the lines below.*

_____ _____ _____ _____ _____ _____

_____ _____ _____ _____ _____ _____

© Topical Resources. May be photocopied for classroom use only.

Name: _____   Date: _____

Making Plurals - Words Ending in 'O'

When making words ending in 'o' plural, add an 's' if there is a vowel before the final 'o' - zoo becomes zoos. **If there is a consonant before the final 'o', add 'es'** - hero becomes heroes. If the word is connected to music then just add an 's'. The word photo also just needs an 's'.

Task 1
Using the above rule, make each of these words plural.

potato		echo	
shampoo		volcano	
piano		photo	
tomato		soprano	
mosquito		igloo	

Task 2
Words ending in ch, sh, s, ss, x or z - to make these plural then simply add 'es'.

Using the above rule, make each of these words plural.

dish →	dishes	bus →	buses
march		pass	
tax		dish	
church		waltz	
fox		guess	
wish		miss	
cake-mix		branch	

Task 3
Pick 12 nouns from your reading book. Make each one plural.

   © Topical Resources. May be photocopied for classroom use only.

Learning Objective: to understand how to change nouns into adjectives.

Name: _____   Date: _____

Changing Nouns into Adjectives

Nouns can be changed into adjectives by adding suffixes.
For example – noise – is a noun, but a **noisy** room – **by adding a 'y' it becomes an adjective**.

Task 1   *Change these nouns into adjectives. You may need to check their spelling in the dictionary.*

Noun	Adjective		Noun	Adjective	
dirt	A	shirt	anger	An	giant
pride	A	boy	sadness	A	story
guilt	A	thief	ugliness	An	troll
courage	A	climber	interest	An	book
hair	A	monster	silence	A	room
beauty	A	princess	coward	A	bully
friend	A	dog	peace	A	playtime
fear	A	rabbit	taste	A	meal
joy	A	song	bump	A	ride
happiness	A	baby	artist	An	picture

Task 2   *Correct these sentences by **changing the noun into an adjective**.*

1. I walked along a danger cliff.
   _____

2. She ate a taste meal.
   _____

3. The baby played with a squeak toy.
   _____

4. Sam bit into a juice pear.
   _____

5. I finished a difficulty sum.
   _____

6. He answered a trick question.
   _____

Topical Resources. May be photocopied for classroom use only.

Name: _____   Date: _____

Revision of Commas in Lists

Commas are used in lists to mark off separate items. A comma is **not needed before the word 'and'**.

For example – The greedy boy ate six cream cakes, two packets of crisps, four packets of sweets and a chocolate bar.

Task 1   *Copy these sentences on to the line below, putting in the missing commas.*

1. At the circus we saw a juggler a trapeze artist and a ring master.
   _____

2. We have been on holiday to France Spain and Germany .
   _____

3. The giant had huge hands long hair and a deep voice.
   _____

4. For my birthday I was given a football a game sweets and a bike.
   _____

5. We made a plane from balsa wood tissue paper and glue.
   _____

6. He painted his picture green red yellow and brown.
   _____

Task 2   *Make up sentences with **commas in lists** using these words.*

1. lunch – fruit a sandwich orange juice and some cake
   _____

2. zoo – seals snakes parrots giraffes spiders
   _____

3. orchestra – violin trumpet flute oboe drums
   _____

4. sandwich – egg ham cheese tuna
   _____

5. playground – see-saw swings slide roundabout
   _____

6. play – princess witch wizard king
   _____

Task 3   *Look through your reading book and find a sentence with commas in a list. Copy it on the line below.*

_____

    © Topical Resources. May be photocopied for classroom use only.

Learning Objective: to understand the use of a colon.

Name: _____ Date: _____

The Colon

A colon is often used to introduce a list.
For example: To make pancakes you will need:
plain flour, butter, eggs, water and milk.

Task 1 *Read the following sentences carefully and **re-write them putting the missing colon in each**.*

1. The newspaper had stories about the following a robbery, a new supermarket and a missing person.
   _____
   _____

2. At the fairground we saw a hoopla stall, a roller coaster and a ghost train.
   _____
   _____

3. We had a school report on these subjects Geography, Science, History and Music.
   _____
   _____

4. At the butchers the lady bought chops, a joint of beef, some sausages and two steaks.
   _____
   _____

5. At Brownies Susie completed badges on cooking, sewing, ball skills and painting.
   _____
   _____

6. My favourite cities are Paris, London, Edinburgh and Madrid.
   _____
   _____

7. To make a sponge cake you will need flour, butter, eggs and sugar.
   _____
   _____

8. Tina played these games Ludo, Snap, Monopoly and Chess.
   _____
   _____

Task 2 *Find an example of the use of a colon in your library book. Copy it here.*

_____
_____

© Topical Resources. May be photocopied for classroom use only.

Name: _____   Date: _____

The Semi-Colon

Semi-colons are used to separate two or more linked clauses. They are **stronger than commas**. They show us that there is a connection between the parts of the sentence.
For example – Sam loves football; Ben prefers rugby.

Task 1   *Read the following sentences and decide where the semi-colon should be. Copy the correct sentence on the line below.*

1. Sam likes pasta Glen prefers curry.

   _____

2. Cats eat meat however cows eat grass.

   _____

3. She opened a bag of hay a rat jumped out.

   _____

4. The castle was empty the only sound was a hooting owl.

   _____

5. Wood is a natural material plastic is man-made.

   _____

6. The taxi did not arrive they had to walk.

   _____

7. Gill likes netball Jon prefers hockey.

   _____

8. I enjoyed PE Sally liked music.

   _____

9. Sammy likes rugby his brother does too.

   _____

10. I like oranges Emma does too.

   _____

Task 2   *Look through your library book. **Find 6 sentences with a semi-colon**. Copy them here.*

_____

_____

_____

_____

_____

_____

    © Topical Resources. May be photocopied for classroom use only.

Learning Objective: to understand the use of dashes.

Name: _____ Date: _____

Dashes

A dash is used to show extra information in a sentence. It has more emphasis than a comma.
For example: Mr Berry is a cook - and a good one too.

Task 1   *Re-write the sentences on the line below putting a dash into each one.*

1. They want to visit London I can understand why.
   _____

2. Ahmed is a swimmer an excellent one at that.
   _____

3. Mrs Smith bakes cakes quite amazing cakes.
   _____

4. The train got us there on time just on time.
   _____

5. Ann made a model most unusual it was too.
   _____

6. The cat won a prize the best in the show.
   _____

7. They visited the gardens a most beautiful design.
   _____

8. Jim painted a picture the best in the competition.
   _____

9. Mr Green made a model castle splendid it was too.
   _____

10. Gerry plays golf a champion he is too.
    _____

11. Carol is a singer the loudest in the choir.
    _____

12. Mr Singh makes up crossword puzzles difficult they are too.
    _____

Task 2   *Now make up three sentences of your own using dashes. Write them here.*

_____

_____

_____

© Topical Resources. May be photocopied for classroom use only.

Name: _____   Date: _____

Hyphens

A hyphen is a punctuation mark which links two words or parts of words to make a single word or expression.
For example – A race over a distance five kilometres could be better described as a **five-kilometre race**.

Task 1   Re-write each of these in a shorter way using a hyphen.

1. A prize of a thousand pounds.   A thousand-pound prize. ____

2. A jug that holds two litres. _____

3. A weight that weighs two kilogrammes. _____

4. A car with three doors. _____

5. A golf course with eighteen holes. _____

6. An interval that lasts fifteen minutes. _____

7. A vase that is heavy at the top. _____

8. A dog with a short coat. _____

9. A lady who works hard. _____

10. A coal that is red hot. _____

11. A cat with fluffy hair. _____

12. A stick that measures two metres. _____

13. A man who is bad tempered. _____

14 A story in three parts. _____

15. A rabbit with long ears. _____

16. A cake with two tiers. _____

Task 2   *Make a collection of some more words which need a hyphen. For example – colour-blind, running-track.*

_____ _____ _____ _____

_____ _____ _____ _____

_____ _____ _____ _____

54   © Topical Resources. May be photocopied for classroom use only.

Name: _____   Date: _____

Speech Marks

Speech marks are used in writing to show the words which are spoken. The words spoken go inside the speech marks. The first word inside the speech marks **begins with a capital letter and the punctuation mark at the end of the speech goes inside the speech marks.** For example – "Come to my house for tea," said Sam. "Thank you," replied Tom.

Task 1   *Put speech marks around the words actually spoken.*

1. Can we play football? asked Rajeev.   2. Be quiet! shouted Mr Smith.

3. I love cats, Sarah said.   4. Miss Jones shouted, Be careful!

5. Jack asked, Can I have a pizza?   6. We painted a picture, said the twins.

7. He is out! shouted Tom.   8. Ahmed asked, Do you like Art?

Task 2   *Re-write the sentences on the line below putting in the **speech marks and punctuation**.*

1. We are going to the cinema said Mary

_____

2. He is playing the piano said Mr Brown

_____

3. They asked Can we come too

_____

4. Ben shouted It's a goal

_____

5. We are going on holiday said the twins

_____

6. Harry asked Did you have fun

_____

7. Go to bed now ordered Dad

_____

8. He is ill said his Mum

_____

Task 3   *Copy two lines of speech from your reading book.*

_____

_____

Topical Resources. May be photocopied for classroom use only.

Name: _____   Date: _____

Proof Reading for Common Punctuation Marks

Task 1   *Carefully **proof read** the following and then **re-write it correctly punctuated on the lines below**. You need **full stops**, **question marks**, **commas**, **speech marks**, **apostrophes** and **a colon**.*

Where are you going Ben asked Mary
Im going to the shop to buy eggs milk butter cheese and ham Dads going to teach me to make an omelette Ben replied
He told Mary about the recipe He said they would need the following four eggs ham chopped into small pieces grated cheese a little milk and some butter to fry it in In a bowl beat the eggs and milk with a whisk Next melt the butter in an omelette pan add the egg then when it is cooked turn the egg mixture over Later add the ham and cheese Finally fold it over into a semi-circle shape
Why dont you have lunch It will be an omelette of course laughed Ben

_____

_____

_____

_____

_____

_____

_____

_____

_____

_____

_____

_____

_____

_____

_____

 © Topical Resources. May be photocopied for classroom use only.

Name: _____   Date: _____

Proof Reading for Common Punctuation Marks

Task 1

*Carefully **proof read the following** and then **re-write it correctly punctuated** on the lines below. You need **full stops**, **commas**, **speech marks**, **question marks**, **exclamation marks** and **apostrophes**.*

Neesha Sally Tom and Meg walked home through the park
Do you think the pond will be frozen asked Sally
Im sure it will be Meg said excitedly
They walked down the High Street round the corner past the church until they came to the Park As they got nearer the pond they heard a scream
What was that asked Neesha
Someones fallen through the ice shouted Sally
Luckily P C Brown was in the Park Sam grabbed a branch and the boy was soon safe
What a silly thing to play on the ice said P C Brown At least hes safe now

_____

_____

_____

_____

_____

_____

_____

_____

_____

_____

_____

_____

_____

_____

_____

_____

_____

Name: _____   Date: _____

Statement and Question Sentences

There are different types of sentences. A **statement sentence tells us some information**. For example – Tony is a tall, twelve year old. **A question sentence asks something**. For example – How tall is Tony?

Task 1   *Answer the following questions in clear **statements or sentences**.*

1. What month is your birthday?
   _____

2. Which road do you live on?
   _____

3. What is your house built from?
   _____

4. Where do you go to school?
   _____

5. Who is your best friend?
   _____

6. What is your favourite meal?
   _____

Task 2   *Write a question sentence about each of these statements.*

1. I enjoy playing netball.
   _____

2. My Grandma is eighty six.
   _____

3. Madrid is the capitol of Spain.
   _____

4. Hedgehogs hibernate in the winter.
   _____

5. St Paul's Cathedral was built by Sir Christopher Wren.
   _____

6. Napoleon was defeated at the Battle of Waterloo.
   _____

Task 3   *Make up two general knowledge questions to ask your friend.*

_____

_____

 © Topical Resources. May be photocopied for classroom use only

Learning Objective: to understand there are different types of sentences.

Name: _____ Date: _____

An Instruction or Command Sentence

An instruction or command sentence asks or tells someone to do something.
For example – Whisk the egg white until stiff.
Often the verb opens an instruction or command sentence.

Task 1 *Here are a set of instructions on how to make a jelly. They are in the **wrong** order. **Cut** them out and **stick them in the correct order. Highlight the verbs in yellow**.*

Allow the jelly solution to set in the fridge for two hours.

Take the jelly out of the packet.

Pour into a jelly mould.

Cut the jelly into cubes using a knife.

Eat the jelly!

Stir until the jelly cubes dissolve.

Place the jelly cubes in a measuring jug.

Add boiling water until the liquid measures a pint

Task 2 *In your book, write instructions explaining how to make scrambled egg.*

Topical Resources. May be photocopied for classroom use only.

Learning Objective: to understand there are different types of sentences.

Name: _____ Date: _____

Exclamation Sentences

An exclamation sentence shows that we feel strongly about something.
It ends with an **exclamation mark** and often *begins* with *what* or *how*.
For example - **How beautiful you look! What a wonderful day!**

Task 1 *Change these statement sentences into exclamations.*

1. The man is tall.
   How tall the man is!

2. The lake is calm.
   _____

3. It is a nuisance.
   _____

4. The bride looks pretty.
   _____

5. It is a wet day.
   _____

6. It is a pity.
   _____

7. The sea is cold.
   _____

8. The statue looks real.
   _____

Task 2 *Change these exclamations into statements.*

1. What rubbish he talks!
   He talks rubbish.

2. How fit you are!
   _____

3. What a wonderful swimmer he is!
   _____

4. How painful is my tooth!
   _____

5. How hard you have worked!
   _____

6. What a bargain it is!
   _____

7. What a great help Mr Brown is!
   _____

8. How peaceful it is!
   _____

Task 3 *Draw a cartoon of a Prince and Princess. Inside a speech bubble write **an exclamation** said by each character.*

  © Topical Resources. May be photocopied for classroom use only.

Name: _____ Date: _____

Writing an Argument

When we write down an argument for or against something, **we use words which help our ideas to be understood clearly**. We also use words which **help us to persuade people of a point of view**. For example -
Using computers is a good thing because people learn more about the world.
Furthermore people may gain a good job in the future because of this.
Or -
Computers are a bad thing since so many children do this rather than read.
Surely it would be more valuable to play with others?

Task 1   *Complete this argument saying that school uniform is a **good idea**.*

I think school uniform is a good thing because _____

_____

_____

Secondly _____

_____

_____

Finally uniform is good because _____

_____

_____

Task 2   *Now complete this argument saying that school uniform is **not a good idea**.*

I think school uniform is a bad thing because_____

_____

_____

Another reason it is a bad thing is_____

_____

_____

Finally uniform is not helpful because_____

_____

_____

Name: _____   Date: _____

Writing an Argument

When we write down an argument for or against something, we use words which help our ideas to be **understood clearly**. We also use words which **help us to persuade people** of a point of view.

For example - **Using computers is a good thing because people learn more about the world. Furthermore people may gain a good job in the future because of this.**

Or -

Computers are a bad thing since so many children do this rather than read. Surely it would be more valuable to play with others?

Task

*Write **two paragraphs**. The first should express the view that **homework is a good thing** for children. The **second** paragraph should express the **opposite** view. Use as many words or phrases in the box below as you can when writing.*

firstly	secondly	because	finally	however	therefore
next	furthermore	finally	surely	on the other hand	

Homework is a Good Thing

_____

_____

_____

_____

_____

_____

_____

Homework Should be Banned

_____

_____

_____

_____

_____

_____

 © Topical Resources. May be photocopied for classroom use only.